Contrary to Parental Belief

Brynn Chisholm

BookLeaf
Publishing

Presentation by *BookLeaf Publishing*

Web: www.bookleafpub.com

E-mail: info@bookleafpub.com

ISBN: 978-93-5761-079-7

First edition 2022

DEDICATION

To my dear Owen, may you always feel loved.

And my darling Thomas, thank you for always being there.

PREFACE

It is here that I apologize for the content ahead. I am not a wordsmith. That being said I've always had an affinity for the spoken word and its ability to transport its reader. My hope is that just one poem speaks to one new mother out there so she knows she's not alone and her feelings aren't abnormal. At its core this book of poems is more of a public journal with artistic flair and it's terrifying to think others will read it, considering the subject matter. Its worth noting that I suffer from post natal depression and anxiety which has painted most of my poems. While they are quite dramatic, being able to write my feelings has helped me process them and I'm on the road to recovery. If you've made it this far, I thank you and I hope you enjoy reading.

The Glow

They told me I would glow

A video of an embryo
Dancing shadows to and fro
Stunned by my amazing show
No one else could possibly know

The know, the know, did you not know?
Who knew it took all this to grow
All the things it needs to flow
To grow your special little glow.

Oh the glow, it comes and goes.
Between the bloat and swollen toes.
Beyond the gifts and tiny clothes.
It lies in wait, it hides, it stows

The glow it seems is not your own
But borrowed from a world unknown
Unknown for now, but time has flown
And shows that you are not alone.

So when you're at your lowest lows,
Tired of tips, and facts, and prose
From seed to sprout and bud to rose
Your little glow still grows and grows.

Born to do

This is what I was born to do.

My biological imperative, my goal, my dream,
my narrative. So, why was I so scared of it?
They say just breathe and so I did.

My lifelong aspiration finally coming to fruition
in a blur of preparations, education, and
fixations.
Despite organization, there was startling
consternation.

Women have been doing this for centuries you
know,
You're not the only one to sow,
You're not the first nor last to grow.

Think of snow, think of rain
Imagine your body welcoming pain
Don't allow fear to fill your brain
Remember the end goal is your gain.

Breathe, push, breathe and hold
hold his hand and bear down slow

Focus, crest, burn and blow,
You've never know relief until that cry eclipses
grief.

You're in disbelief.

A weight on your chest, the best, a moments rest
between the stress and mess.
The journeys end, but no, the start!
Your heartbeat suddenly pulled apart.
A part of you, your piece of art
Your hearts echo and counterpart

The Blur

Lights, beeps, white sheets.
Poles, and tubes and plastic seats.
Foggy transitions and bloody secretions
A little blue bundle, near bottles and teats.

I am a shell. A husk. A ghost
Sleep only 1 to 2 hours at most
nameless well wishers come calling in clusters
I lie, I can't wait to play host

Home, at last, the final rung
My prized parcel protected, to my dearest I
clung.
Sunbeams spotlight my new life's ambition
I seesaw from lifeless to strangely high strung

Stinging and weeping
Oozing and dripping
My body's not mine as I drag it from sleeping

swaddles and screams
Burp cloths and creams
Nappies upon nappies, an endless fever dream.

Baby Blues

Don't think too much or else you'll cry
No need to waste more tears
Think all the time or else he'll die.
I'm stuck inside my fears

Sleep when the baby sleeps
And cook when baby cooks
Sweep when the baby sweeps
Its harder than it looks

Emotions sitting at their peak
waiting to push through,
Can't bring myself to even speak
They call it baby blues

How does everyone do this?
Feeling overwhelmed and lost
I'm at the depth of an abyss
I wish I'd known the cost

Do what's best for you.
No, do what's best for baby,
Relationship, family, development too
Not allowed to say maybe

Be calm and never stress
Because your mood will affect him
Make a plan, don't just guess
The future feels so grim

Every choice is wrong and right
I've failed my little one
Wishing for each coming night
Dreading each new sun.

These blues I hope will turn to green
Lush, growing, and vibrant
Of all the colours to be seen
This one's a moody tyrant

The Trope

What can be said that hasn't already been said

Your giggle makes the world go round
Your eyes an artists dream
Pudgy feet to stomp the ground
Downy skin of cream

Amaze me daily with your skill
Learning lightning fast
To share your laughter and your thrills
Each greater than the last

Fairer than Adonis
And spirited as a sprite
Ne'er the gods have ever seen
A babe of such delight

You've so much life ahead of you
To touch, explore and see
I want to show it all to you
But you won't always have me

You'll surpass those who critise
Your strength will vanquish all

Your light will outshine friend and foe
You'll never trip or fall

Then again...

Perhaps my forecast of your future
Might be slightly biased
As long you're content in life
You'll sit amongst the highest

The Slow Burn

Hit me while I'm down,
Wake me when I sleep.
Hurt me when I ache
And watch me while I weep.

Show me your relentlessness
Show me your persistence
Show me your exasperation
Show me your resistance

Don't look at me my son
I can't look back at you
Not because you're not a gift
But because my joys are few.

Dependent on my sleeplessness
Feeding off my tears and sweat
This stranger laying in my arms
I do not know you yet

You must be so in love with him
My family would voice
I glance at him, worn and numb
Guess I don't have a choice

Is he a good baby? Sleeps all night?
The masses always ask
"He's great", i say, "perfect" I act
While I hide behind my mask

But how could I possibly
be sad at a time like this?
I got exactly what I dreamt
I should be fraught with bliss

The days are long the nights moreso
My cup is seldom full
My mind is twisted, twined in knots
Thick and hot as wool

The gruelling labour that it takes to
Mend your mind and soul
Takes more time than you've to spare
And daily takes its toll

But through the fog, a glint of light
Faint and far away
Urges me to carry on
To get me through each day

Truthfully my boy
My love for you has been a trial
But it's not stopped growing, never slowing
Since your first sweet smile.

Help me I'm fine

Tell me what to do
But don't tell me how to do it
I'm the only one who can
No, please walk me through it

Take this baby far away
But not away from me
I want to stay here in my nest
I want to fly away free

I need a break, I need some space
I need him on my chest
I need to watch him as he sleeps
I need a good night's rest.

My love is torn between two men
But sadly one must wait
He waits for touch, he waits for praise
He waits to be a mate.

I need a hand but not from you
I'd hate to be a bother
I don't need anyone, I'm ok
I need my mother and father.

The slightest cry beckons me
To hasten to his side
Do I sleep or eat or wash?
Too drained to dare decide.

A willing servant, broken slave
The burden is all mine
But I wouldn't be anywhere else
Please help me I'm fine

Slumber

Suckling lips, pure and soft
Nuzzle to my chest
Snuffled snores through button nose
Cheeks pressed against my breast

An angel face of warmth and grace
Porcelain velveteen.
This peachy cherub; tender prince
Sleeps flawless and serene

Resentment

Gnawing, grating, unabating
Swirling through my head unwavering
Red hot seething, clenching teeth and
Wondering where the hell you've been

The world around is muffled, my eyes are fixed
and glazed.
Hes being slack, stop keeping track,
Feels like I've been here for days.

Where is his initiative
Why can't it mimic mine?
Hes tired too, worked all day through
Hes been doing overtime.

But he get breaks, he goes outside
He eats uninterrupted,
He drives in silence, chat with friends,
When was he disrupted?

I've slept 2 hours since yesterday
My breasts are chapped and sore
I haven't shower in 4 days
Exhausted to my core.

Why's this burden all on me?
Why did I choose this path?
Some days it feel like it's too much
Forgive me for my wrath

Should

It seeps with haughty arrogance,
It peppers friendly talks
Its judgement makes you doubt yourself
It locks you in a box

It chews you up and spits you out
It jeers "you've chosen wrong!"
You've done the research how could you
Have missed this all along!

It sneers and mocks; ignores your pride
Puffs up in condescension
Patronising, pulverising
You wished it wasn't mentioned.

As if I haven't tried all that
Like its not been my mission
Well intentioned it may be
Next time just stop and listen.

A Parent's Lullaby

Cotton candy skies fade away
Dusk settles in its place
Crickets sing, an ambient hum
Stars twinkle deep in space

Moon beams kiss decluttered benches
hush descends upon the house
Balmy breeze from open windows
A playful squeeze from your spouse.

A steamy shower, whiffs of flower
Lotion in your hands
Empty soiled laundry baskets
No one making demands.

Spotless gleaming high and low
No dirty dish in sight
A favourite treat between your lips
A blanket wrapped around tight

A gentle snore behind closed doors
A new book on the chair
Feet propped up off clear floors
Small pleasures rich and rare.

Enjoy Every Moment

You're discontent you've gotta vent about the extent of your lament. Enjoy every moment.

you don't feel present. Energy spent, you're pent up and bent out of shape. Enjoy every moment

Top up supplement, repetitive feeding event, trying hard not to resent. Enjoy every moment.

But it's well-meant, try to be pleasant.

Enjoy every moment

Who is she?

She wears high heels
Drinks wine for fun
Wears tight dresses
Stays out till the sun

Jet-setting diva
Courage to soar
Endless new friends
Selfies galore

Adventure awaits her
She off like a flash
Indulgent and daring
Shes got spending cash

Waist like a model
Natural and young
Vivacious and funny
Seldom high strung

Accomplished and driven
At peak physique
Resourceful, resilient
New plans every week

Mirror's reflection
The past is a blur
Now I sit and I stare
at what remains of her

Sensitive

Exposed like a nerve, Electrical stabs from
innocent jabs.

Words poking holes in my paper thin skin, but
I'm the one letting it in. The idle chatter that
blathers it shatters and why the hell do I feel like
it matters.

Can't stop ruminating how the worlds
desintegrating, it's devastating. Every second
passed another casket. My empathy's too much
for me, the weight, the intensity, limits and
upsets me.

My imagination's paralysing. Overanalysing and
emphasising the risks and fears, the threats and
tears. Im frozen. The route I've chosen is filled
with doubt.

Everywhere there's loss, everywhere there's
sorrow. Somewhere someone's wishing for
tomorrow.

I wish for armour, for ardour, for my strength the ward off the shoulds and what ifs and coulds and tiffs.

 I'm sensitive, but I don't wanna be I gotta be level-headed not offended. Be realistic instead of this ballistic cynic, this pessimistic skeptic.

The Park

23

Pink stained cheeks from watermelon kisses
Coconut sunscreen permeates the air.
A parade of hats, and shorts and sandals
Water and mats and snacks at the ready
Sunrays speckle and tingle my shoulders but the
breeze cools me again.
Rumblings of far away traffic and bustling trees.
Tickling grass and dirty finger nails.
Jingling chains from occupied swingsets
Screams of joy heard for miles around

Chaos

Where's this laundry coming from
How come you've got no clothes?
What's this wet stuff on the ground
Don't stick that up your nose

Where'd you find a socket wrench
What's stuck under this chair?
Stop running in the house I said
Go outside! Get some fresh air!

How much yogurt is there left?
Snack time will be soon
I think the good bread is on sale
Here's your favourite spoon

Don't do that, I told you no
I'll say it once again
You can wait til after dinner
How will I lift this stain?

This carpet needs a vacuum
This bill needs to be paid
Put it away after you're done!
I should hire a maid

How'd you get your hair this way?
Lets run through a comb
Suddenly comes a familiar sound
Daddy's finally home

The cycle - A Haiku

Change always happens
I've finally found my stride
Here we go again

Rekindled

He takes my hand and pulls me in
At first I hesitate, uncertain what's needed of me.
Nothing is needed.
I melt into his familiar hold.
My chin slips into its place on his chest.
I breathe him in for the first time in months. We
share a moment of peace.
I'm flooded with memories of a different me.
But he remains the same.
It's been so long since I've felt his body against
mine, and I instantly realise how much I've
missed it.
His stubble tickles my face playfully, it reminds
me of the smile the hides beneath.
I feel safe and secure.
I exhale my tension and worry.
I am brought back to square one. We are one. I
feel like myself again, if even for a moment.
His strong hands brush my hair aside and kiss
my cheek gently. His kind eyes tell me that
everything is going to be ok.

I love you, he says. And I believe him.

New Body

She hangs around in corners
Hiding from the light
She dresses down and dark and drab
She remains out of sight.

I see a glimpse of her dragging feet
Pulling her bulky frame
She droops and slouches everywhere
It really is such a shame

The tiger stripes that grew upon
Her loose and homely belly
Can never fit her clothing right
And jiggles about like jelly

Despite these flaws her body moves
Her legs are sturdy and strong
Her baby feels safe within her arms
It's there where he belongs

My body isn't what it was,
And never will be again
But as long as it's good enough for him
I'll hold him until then

Perseverance

The kitchen may be messy
Every toy on display
Laundry piled up at the stairs
But you've made it through the day

Dinner was bits of bread and cheese
They don't eat what they should
Tomorrow is another day
You did the best you could

They cried and screamed for hours
I know some days it's tough
You're stronger than you think
You are always enough

You make them feel forever loved
They don't see the mayhem
They see a safe and warm embrace
You are everything to them